Karrie Ross

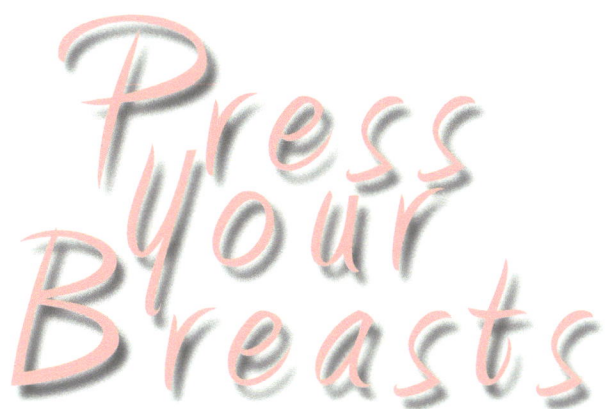

April 2015

Press Your Breasts
by Karrie Ross

Copyright © 2015 Karrie Ross

Karrie Ross
12516 Washington Place, Los Angeles, CA 90066
Visit our website at www.KarrieRoss.com.

Printed in the United States of America

Book Design by Be It Now! Karrie Ross

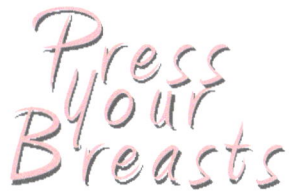

I believe the best way to create a happy healthy self is to attend to the internal energies that are developing in us all the time, the act of observing and listening to them at any given moment.

This is not the first series where I explore breasts… it is the first time I'm using my breasts as the main element in an art project… "Press Your Breasts." A part for me is in the sharing of my experience, the internal beauty of breasts with others, some who may have had illnesses, cancer, and lost their breasts. I am in process of expanding this concept into gallery exhibitions and fund raising opportunities for non-profit use. Please contact me if any part of this new project resonates with you.

From a purely process driven position, the mono print has been turning up in my work now for the past year mostly as a bleep of color flying around the images in the pieces adding an energy that can not only be seen but felt.

Why my breasts? Why NOT my breasts? As I head into the next twenty or so years of my life, I'm 65 years old right now, I figure I might as well explore things I didn't when I was younger. What we learn as we age is that we have a set point for age-consciousness … mine is 5 years old! So all I want to do is play, and I chose to play with my breasts and paint.

So I found some paper, prepped my palette, cleaned my brushes, prepped my breasts, logged into my iphone and started painting, shooting video and stills and pressing my breasts to paper and canvas with a wonderful feeling of exploration and tingling inside. I am really liking this mono print thing and might expand it to other parts of my body.

I'm scared shitless! Artists are supposed to bring things to light, to expose, to share an exploration, a why? So, while others are exploring politics, economics, and environmental issues, I'm exploring my internal world — my image of self — for as I think I am, I am, and as long as I have an inquiry as to who, what, where, when, how, why I am — I will explore and share my internal questions and insecurities — and be a fearless OMG example of living my art with abandon.

My previous book, *My Breasts Talking* is a narrative about my breasts', observations and the interesting conversations that occur. They are expressive and definitely have a voice that is unique… you know, one that stands out from the rest of the body.

My *Bustiers* are a sculpture series (using plastic bra forms) and is about the beauty we show the world (the front side), and the internal dialogue and feelings we have (the back side).

+ + +

Karrie's work centers around the personal generation of a continuous flow of energy and her belief that this energy can be shared with the world through exploring — art, haikus, writing, music, and exampling the concepts of feng shui. energy balancing, and most of all PLAY.

Karrie is a native of Los Angeles and describes herself as visual artist who creates art with abandon.

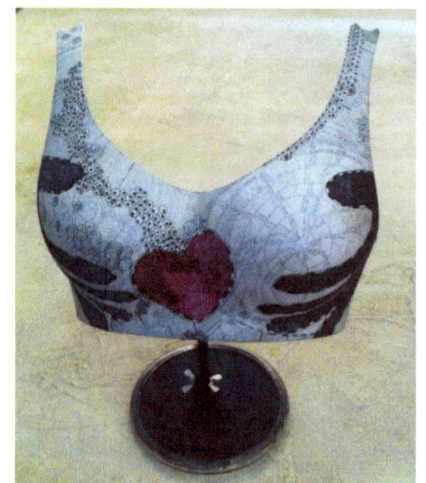

MY BREASTS TALKING — "If your body could speak, what would it say?" is what author/fine artist Karrie Ross answered when asked "Why she wrote the book?" then she went on to say, "This all started when I was considering what to paint next and I decided to apply my Spiral Series look to a plastic bra form. As I began painting and drawing on the form, the front, of course, was where I put all my attention and creativity.

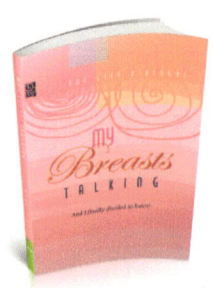

I was happily on my way to finishing off the fourth one. When I turned it around to sign it, like I'd done the three previous ones, the aha of the blank back caused me to question what I could put there. After long consideration, I arrived at the realization that "the front is what I show to the world and the back reflects my internal thoughts." WOW! and the rest is history. Available at amazon.com

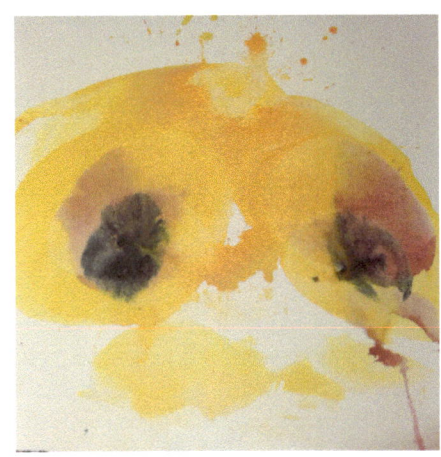

The following artworks are watercolor
mono prints using my breasts pressed
to paper or 4"x4" canvas. there were
no brush strokes used except when
applying the paint to the breasts.

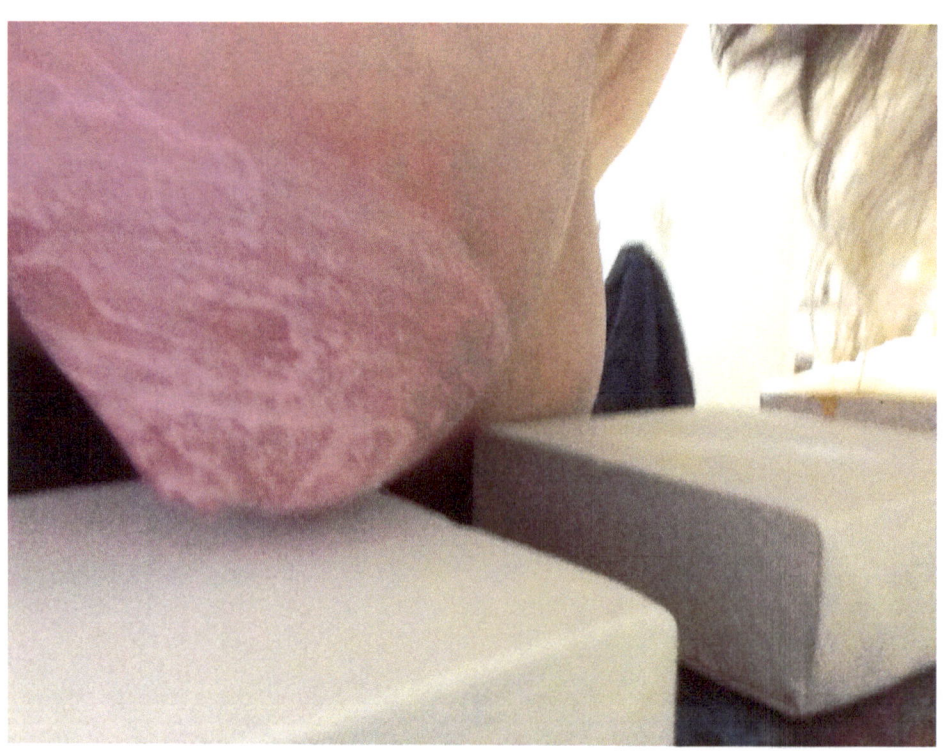

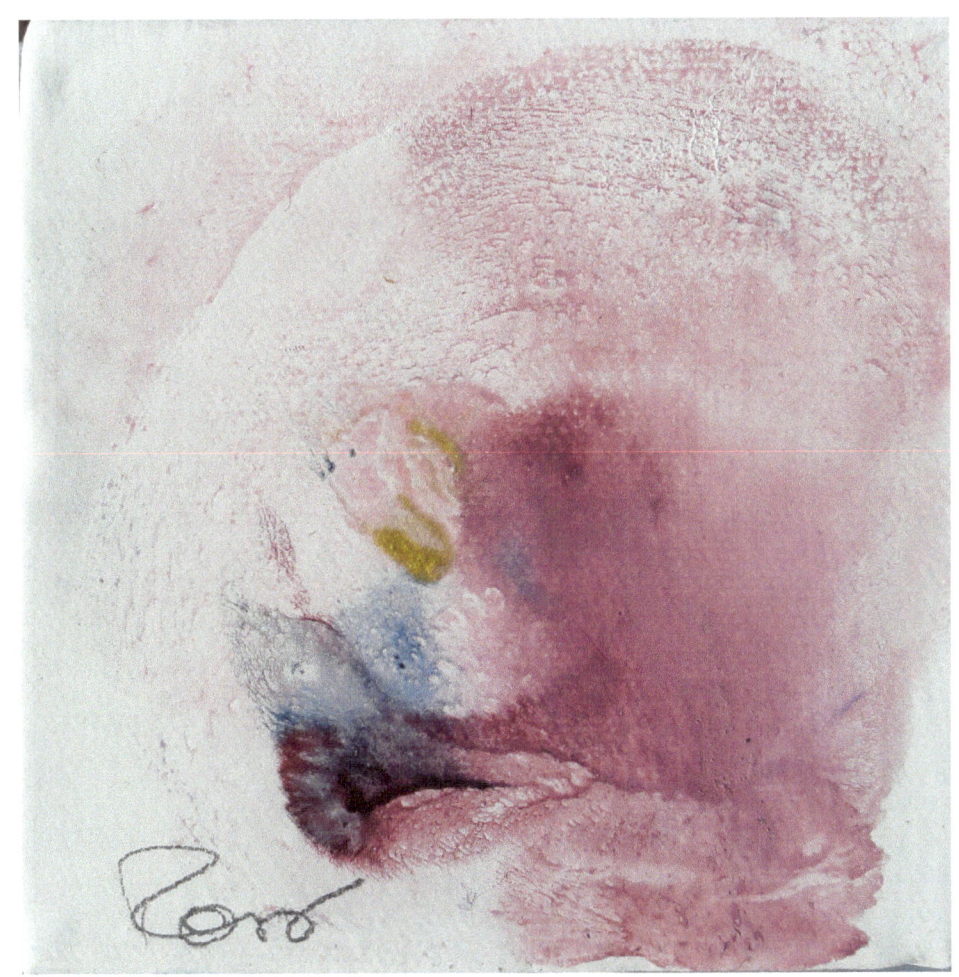

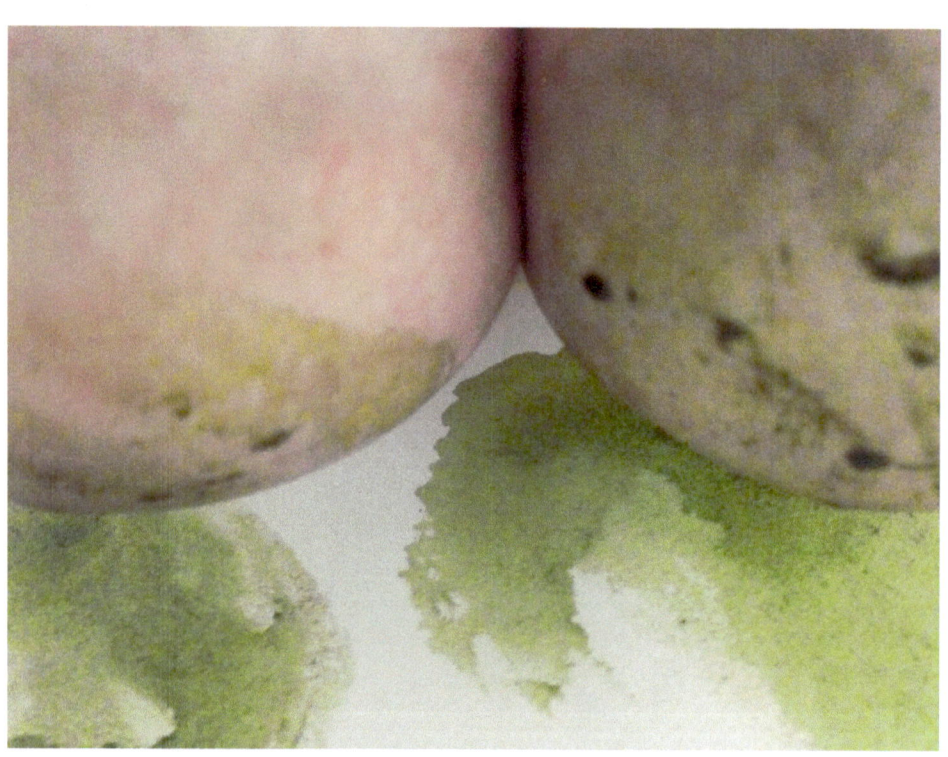

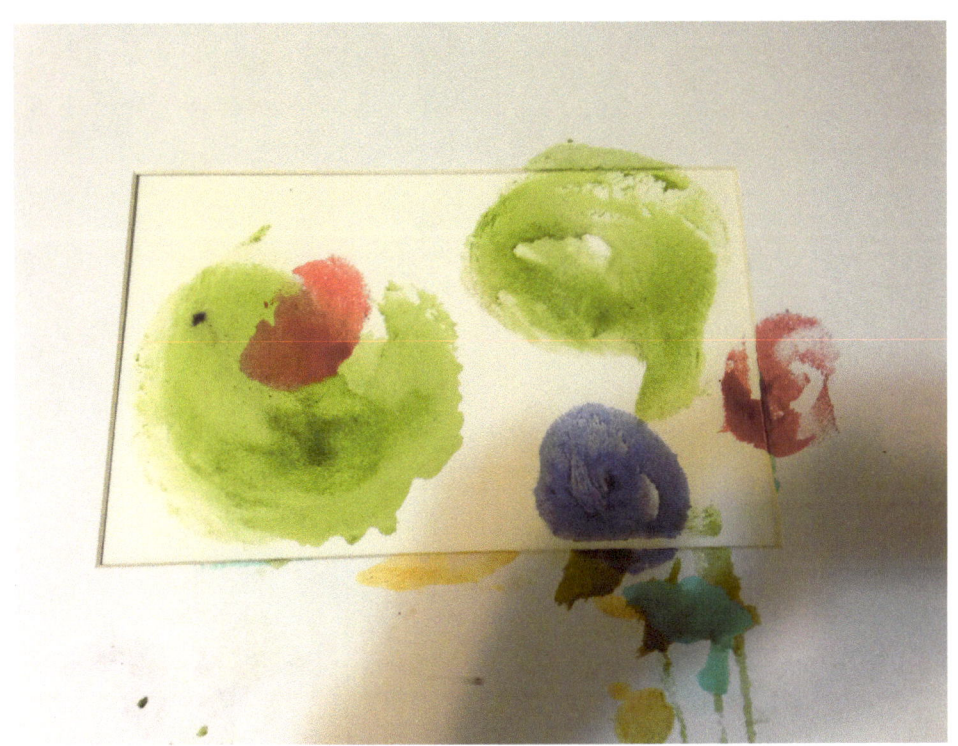

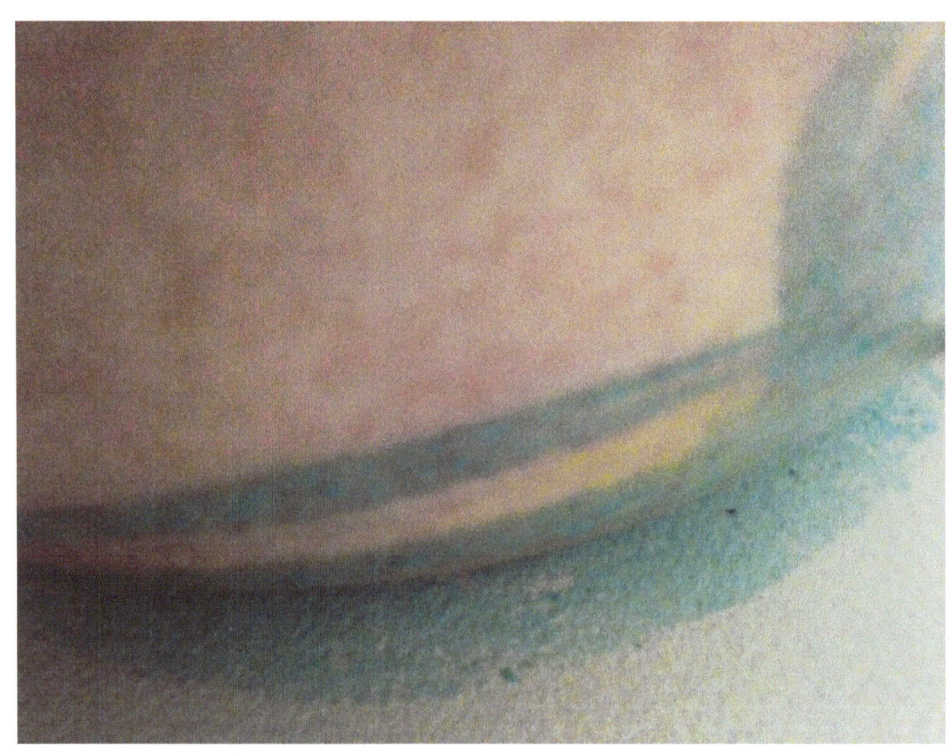

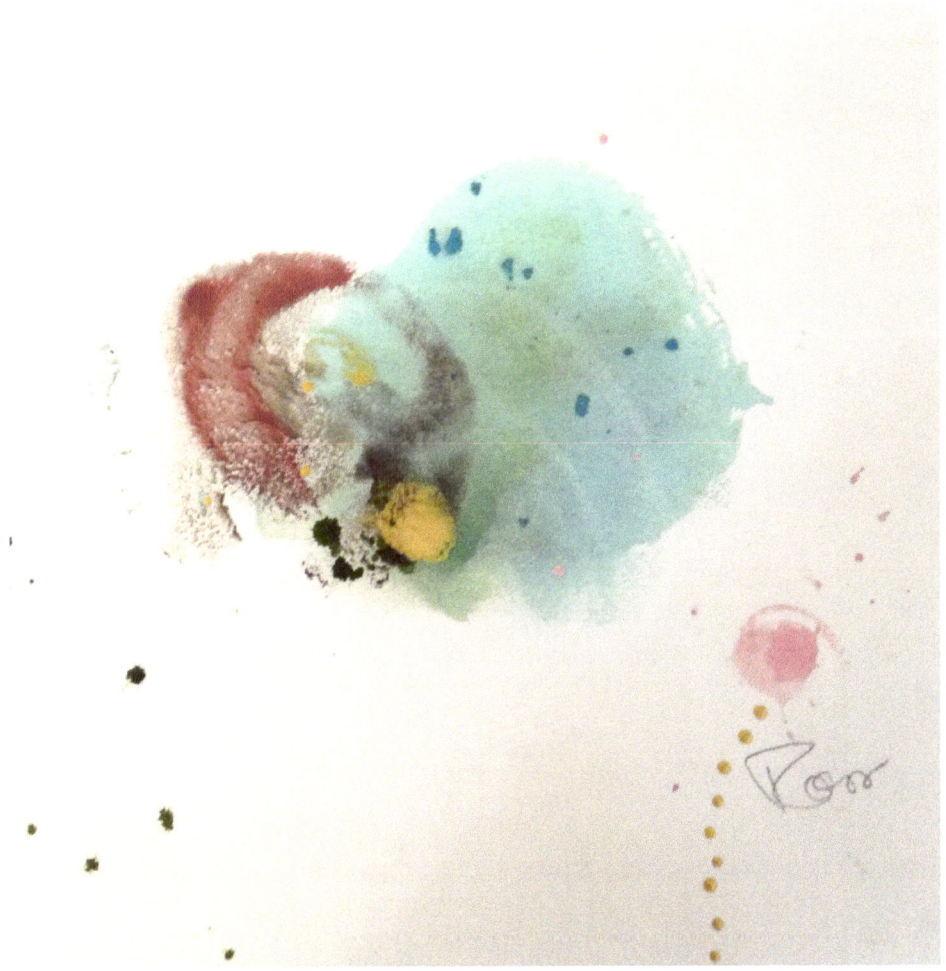

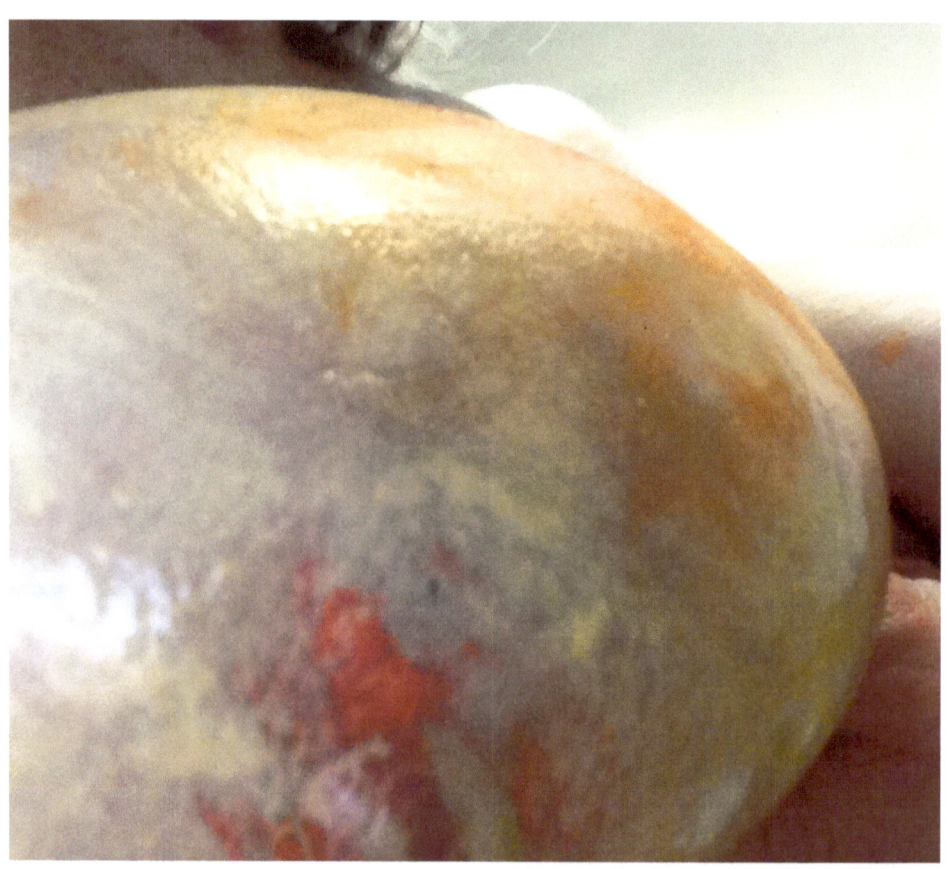

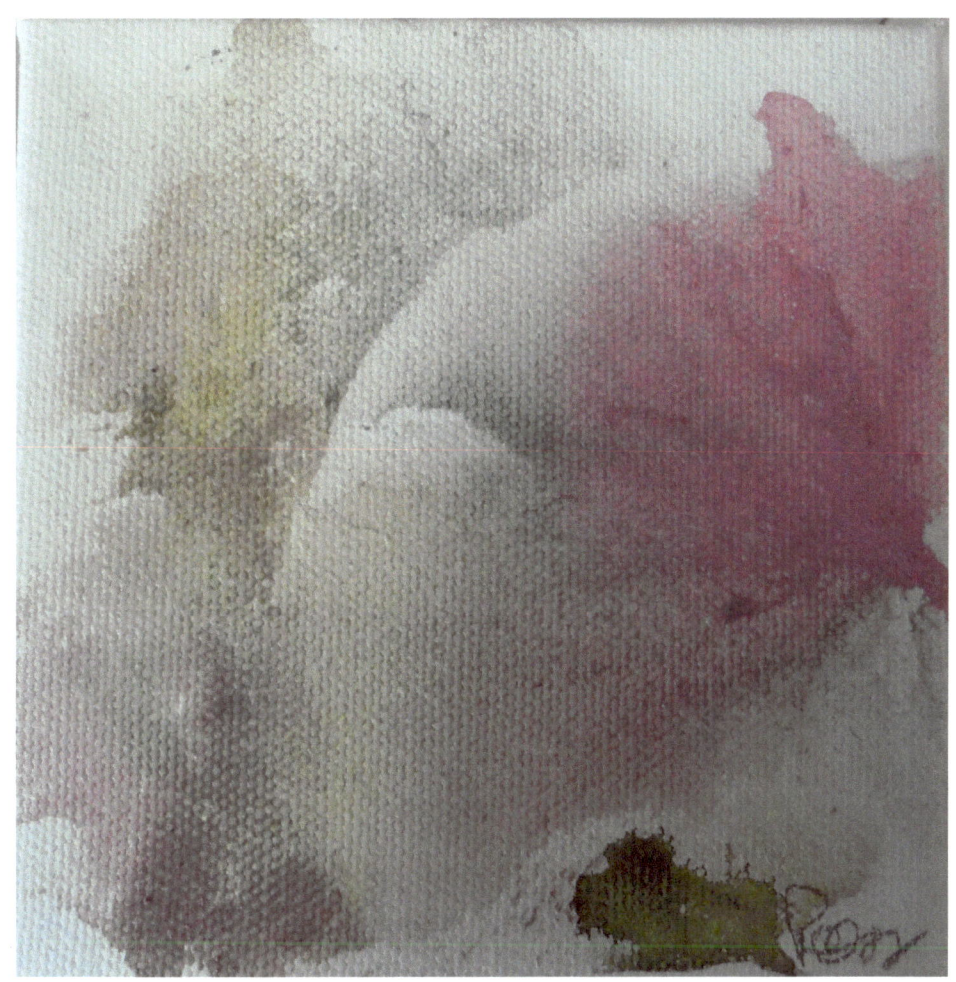

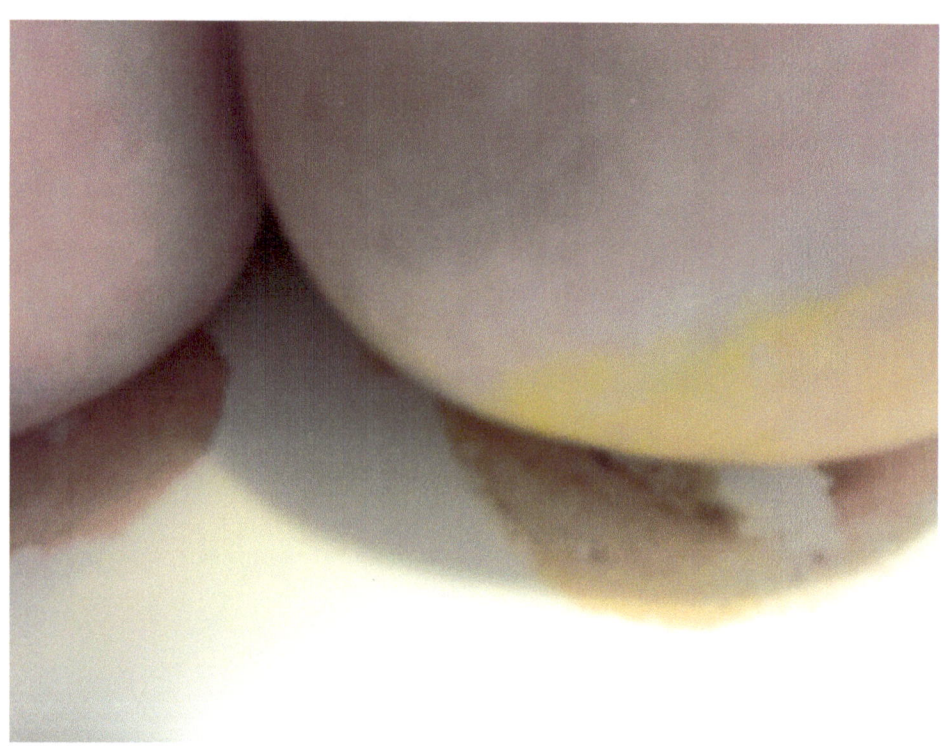

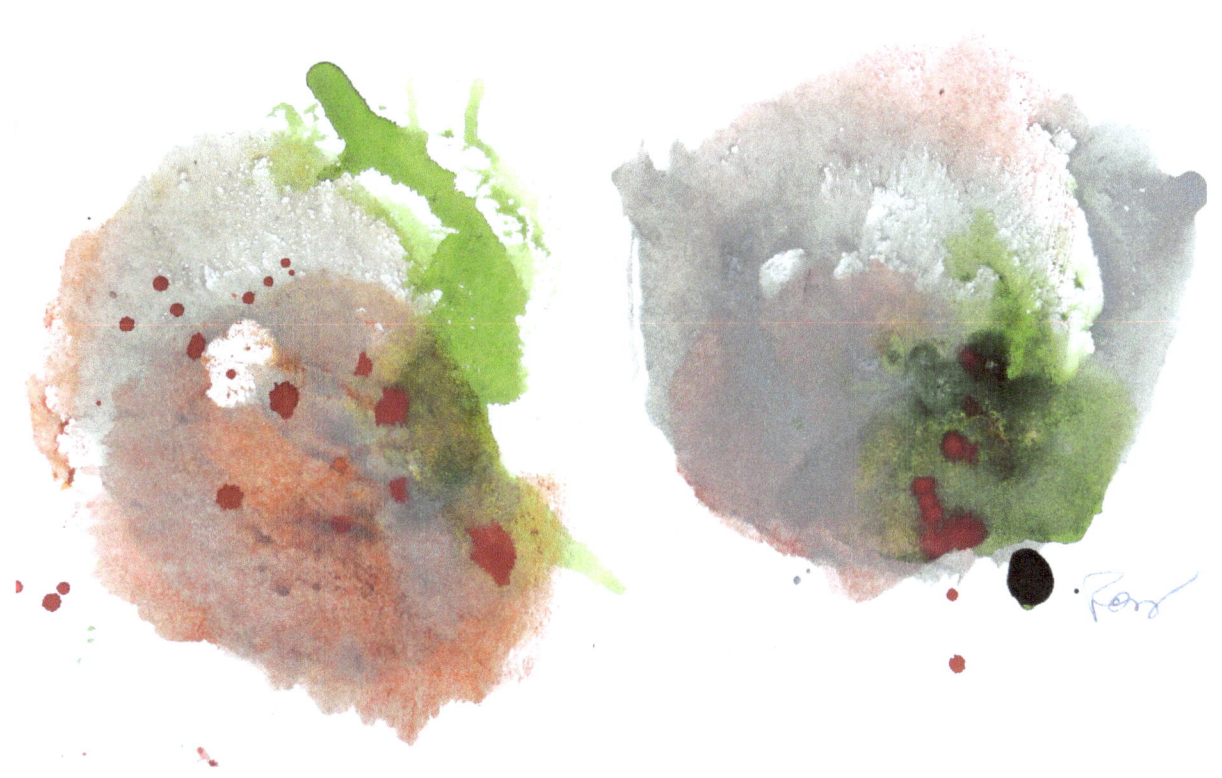

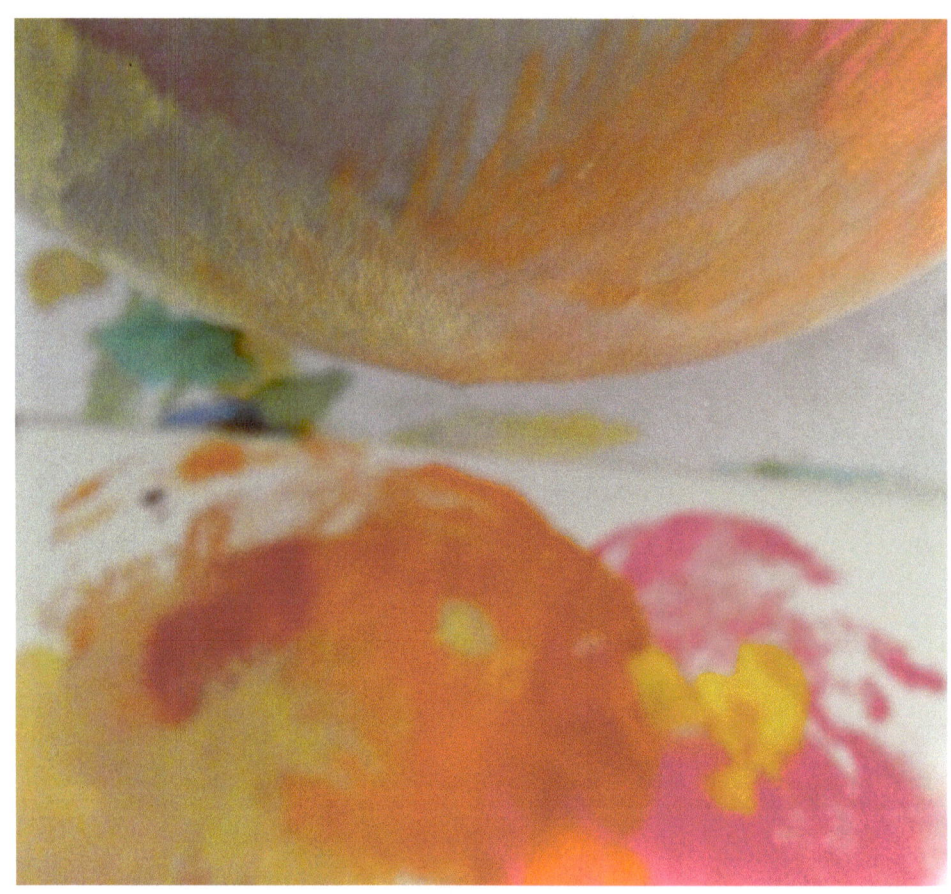

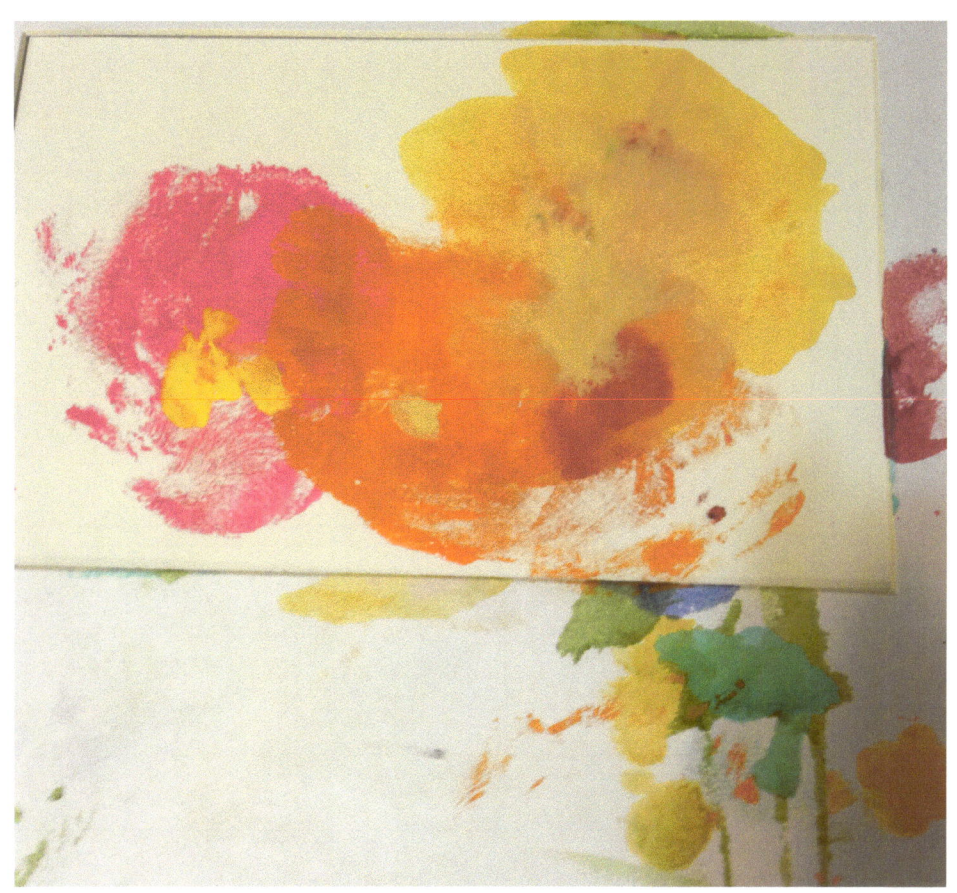

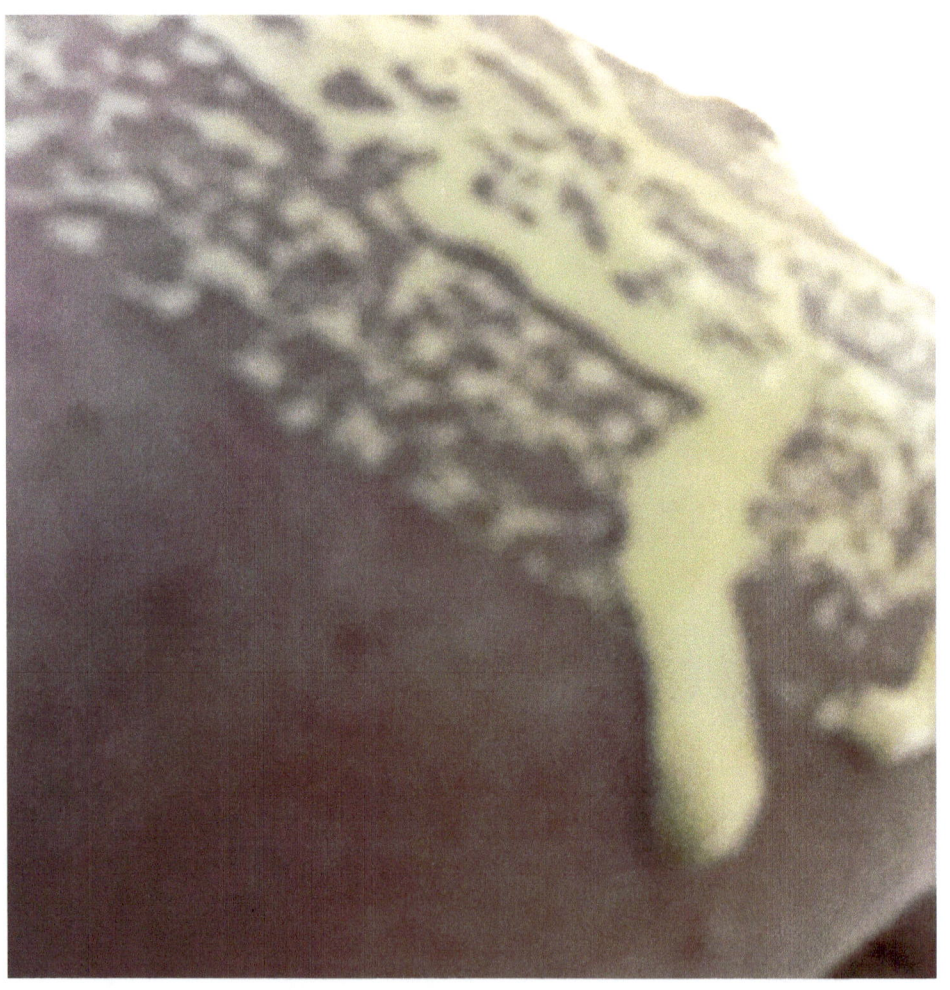

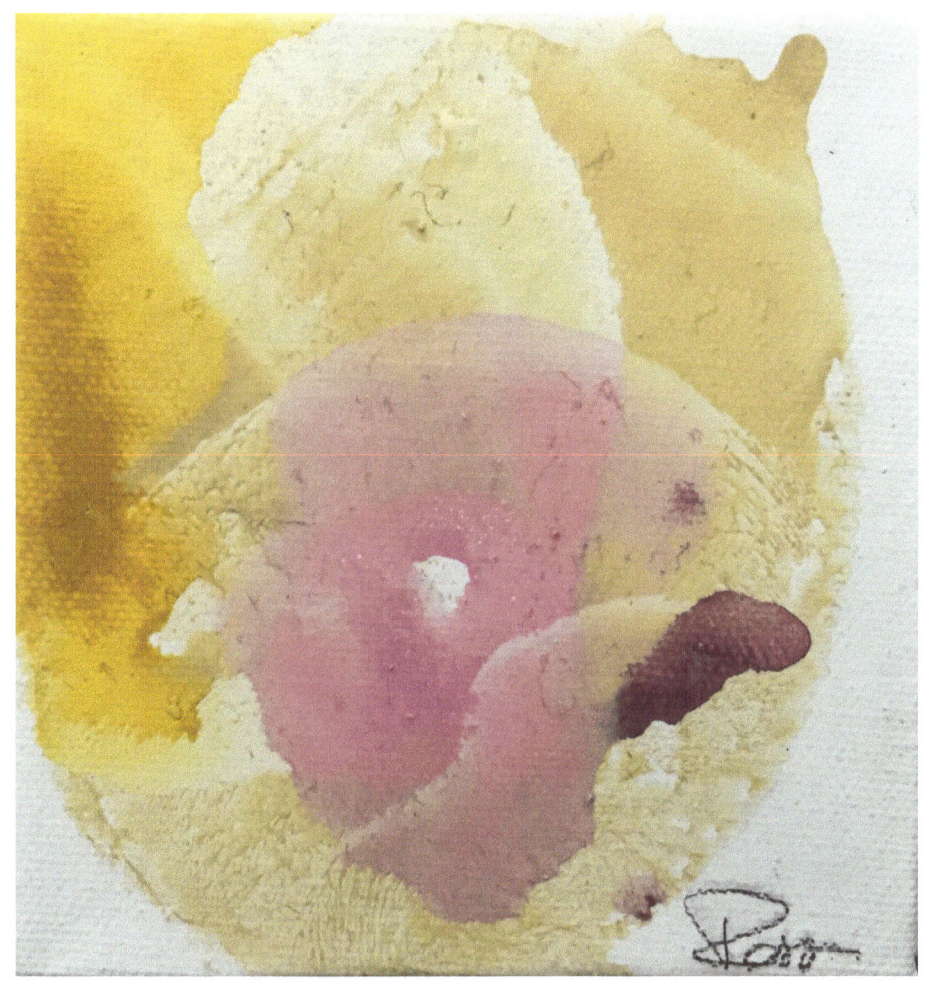

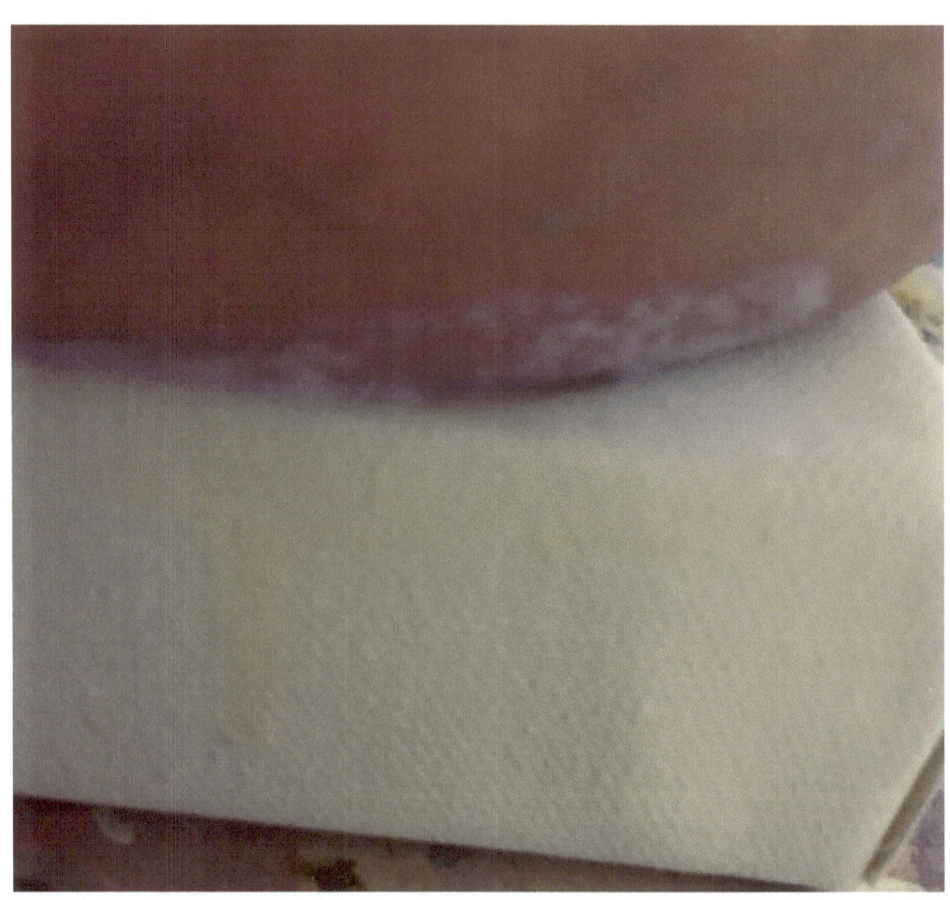

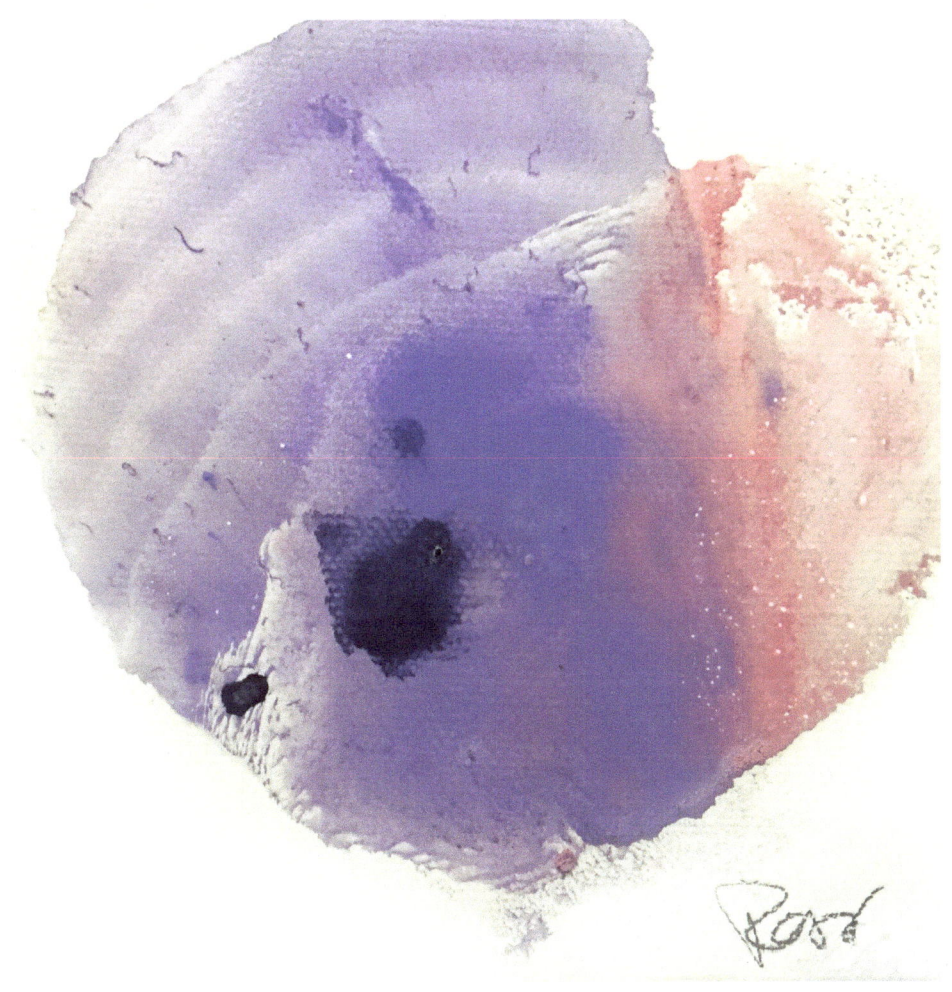

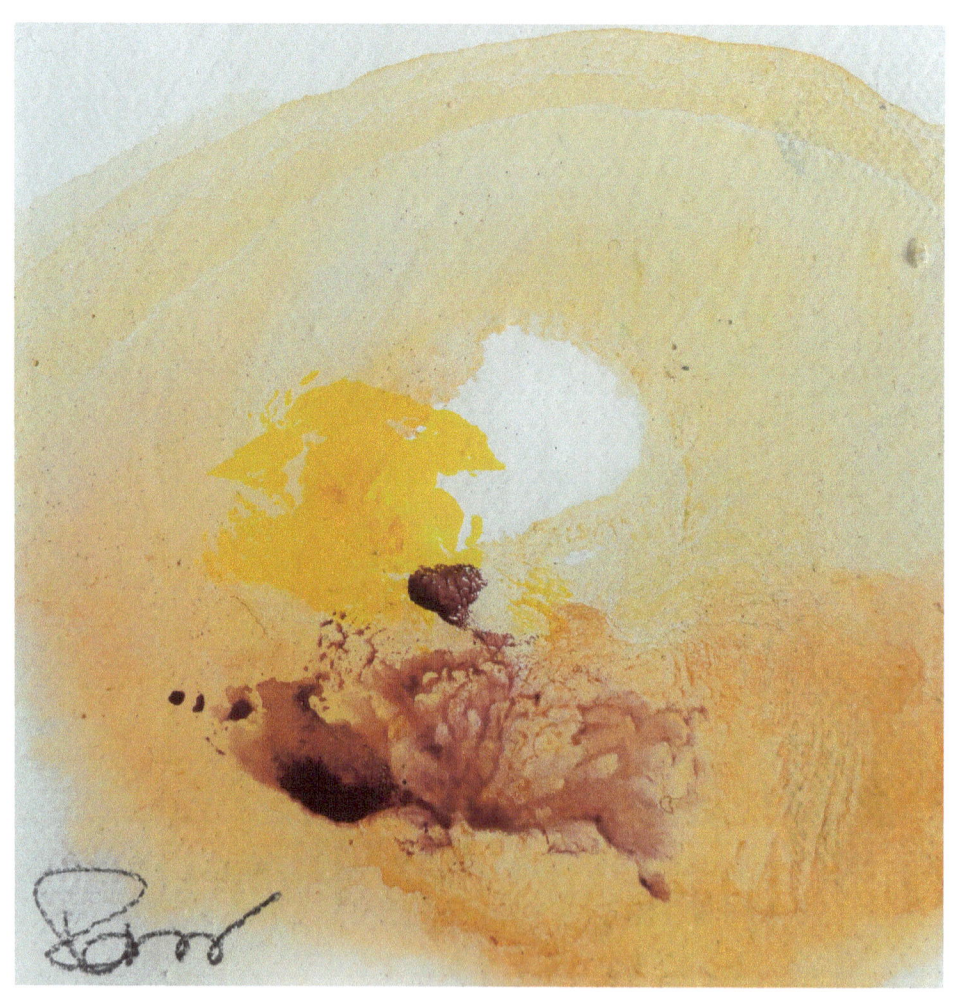

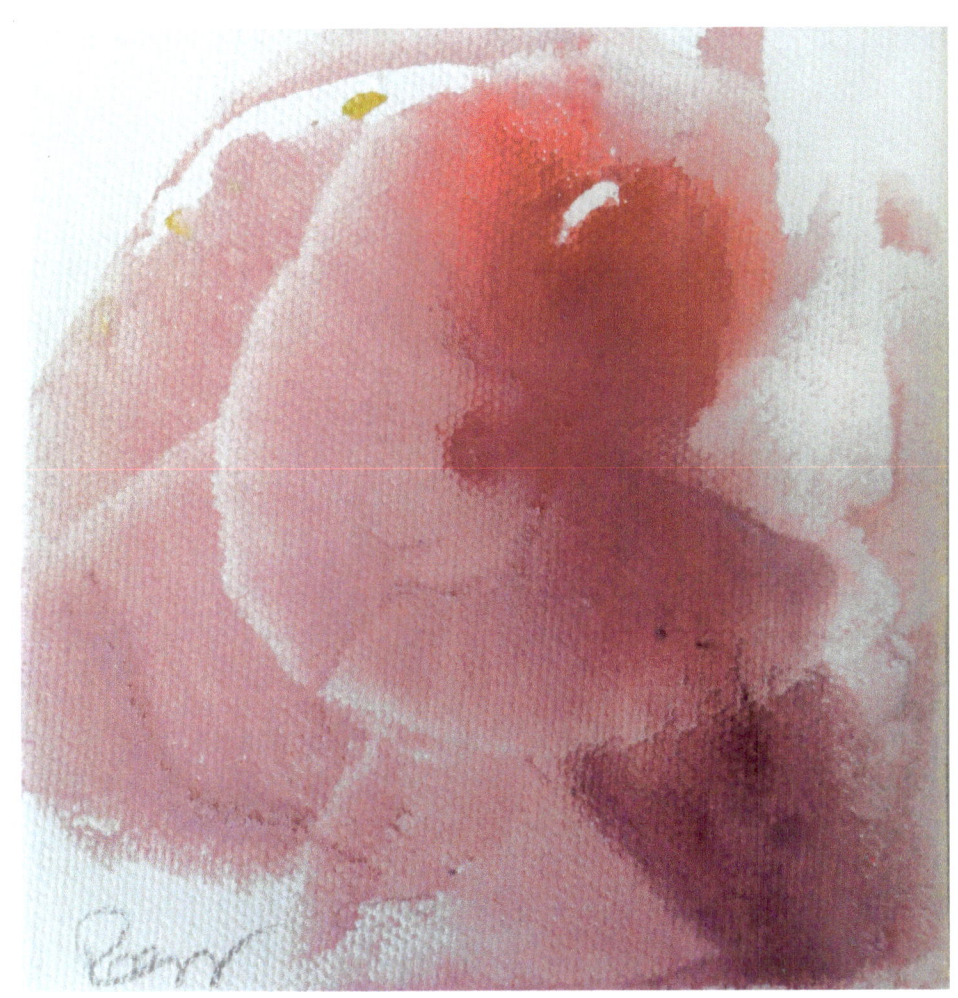

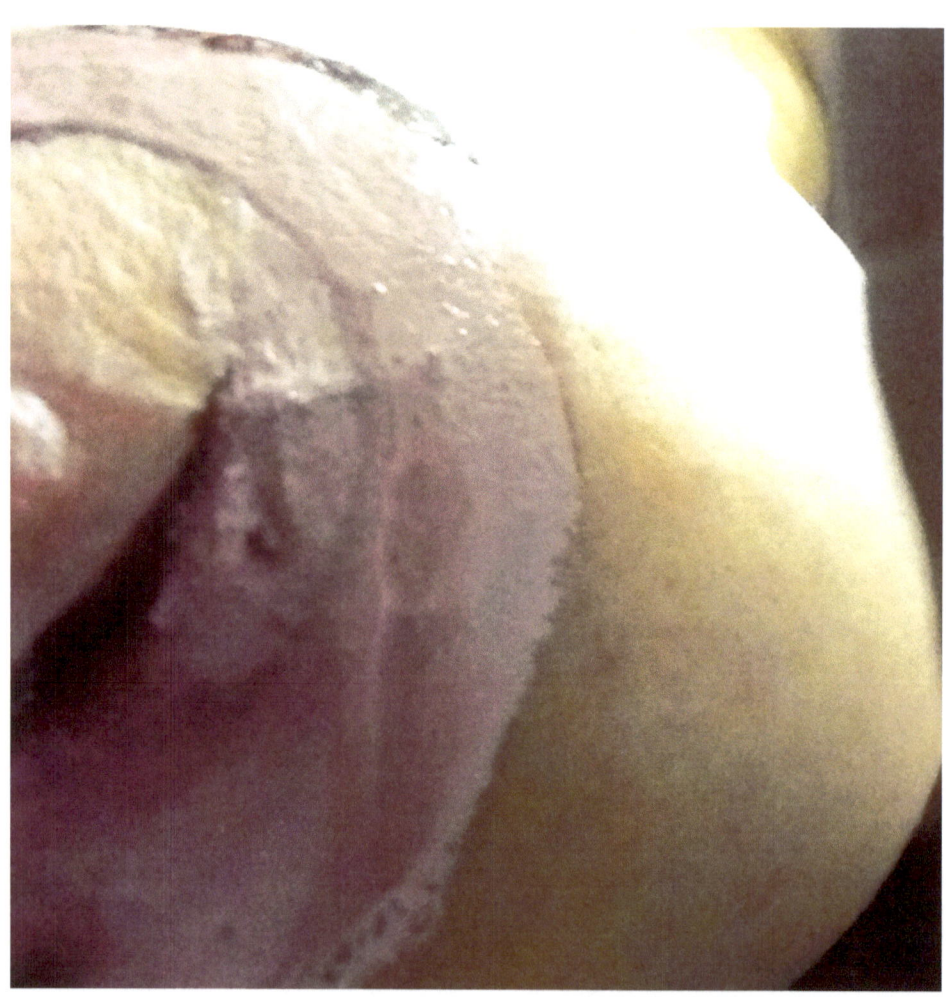

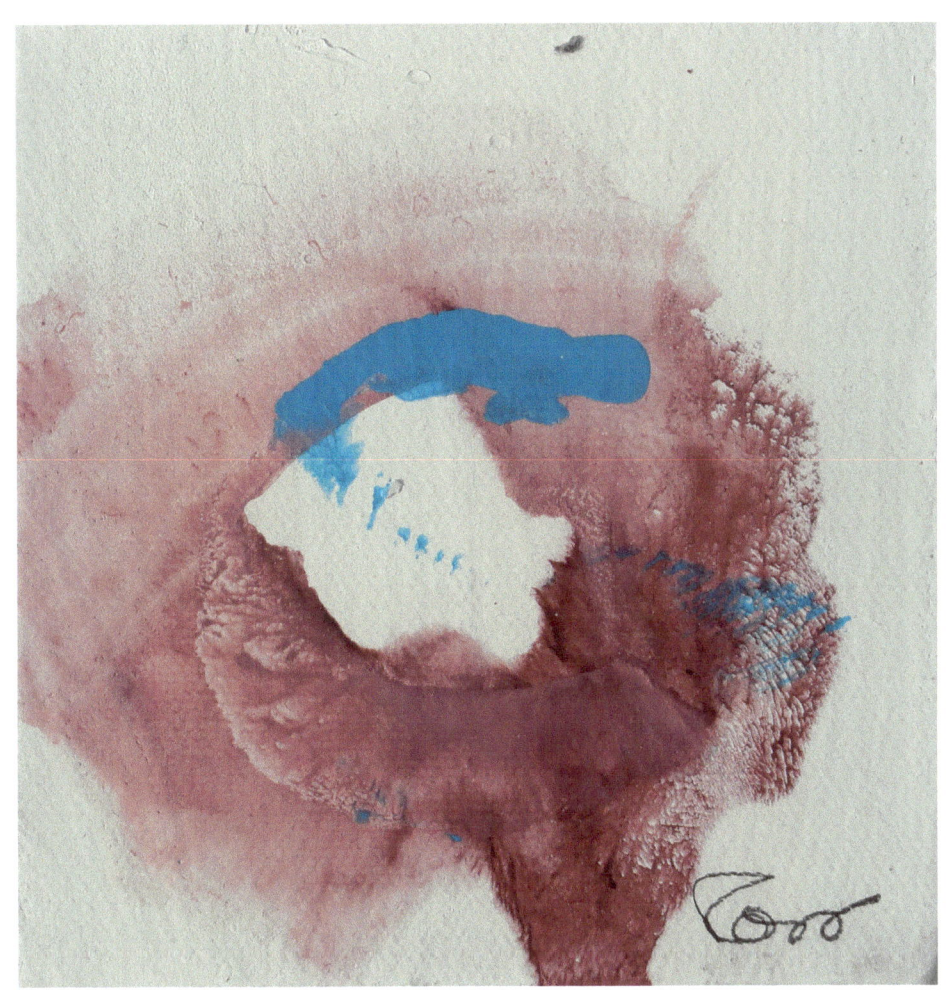

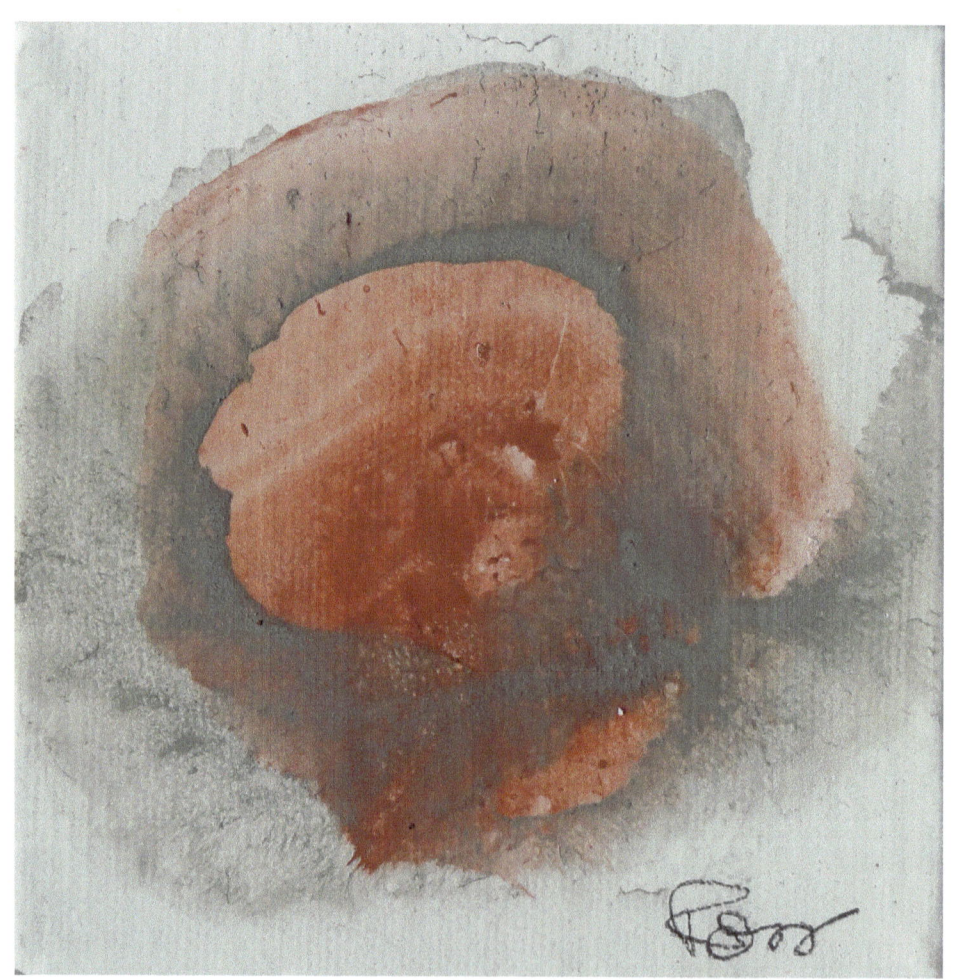

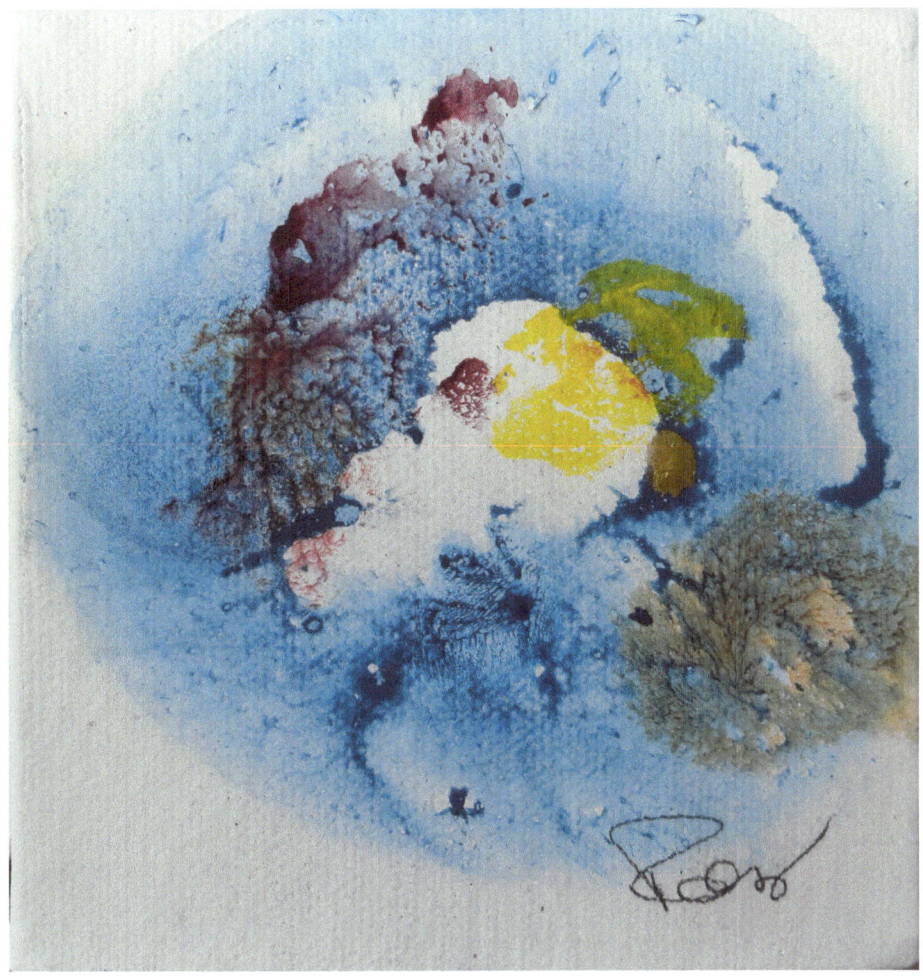

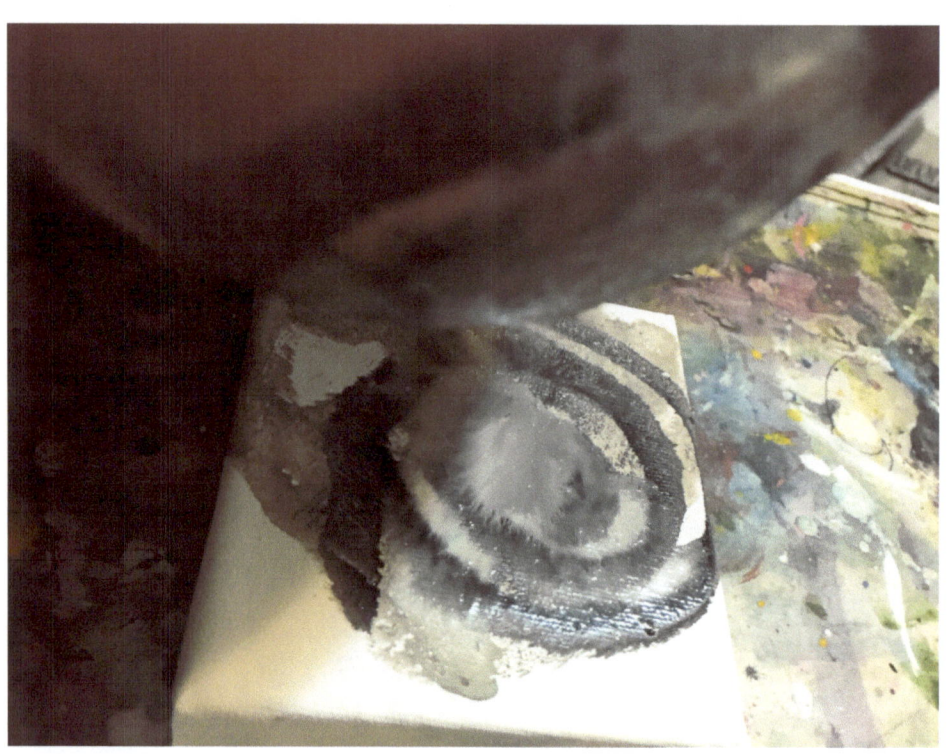

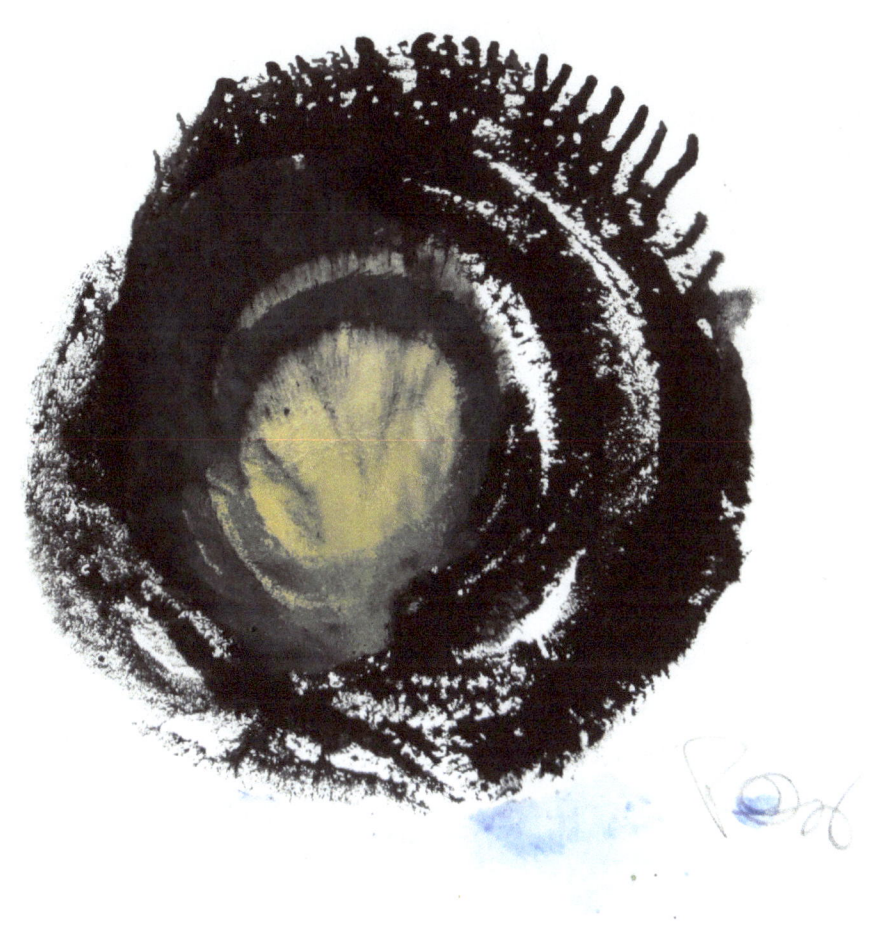

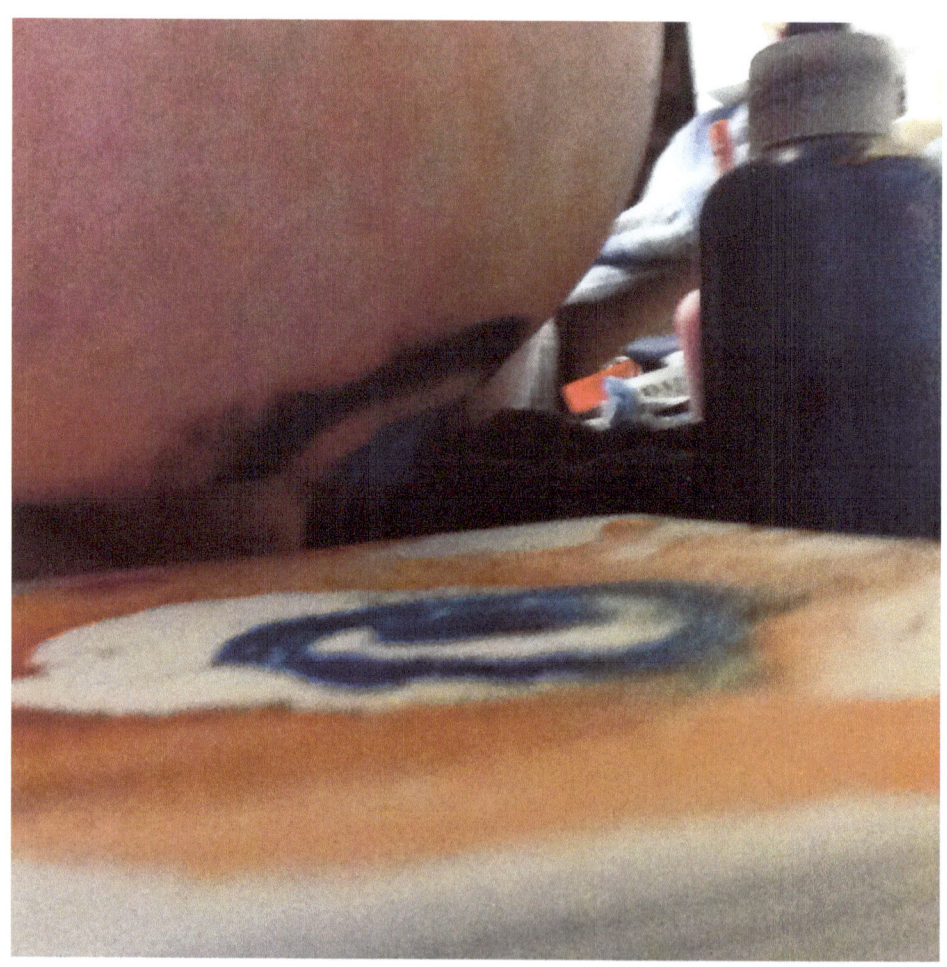

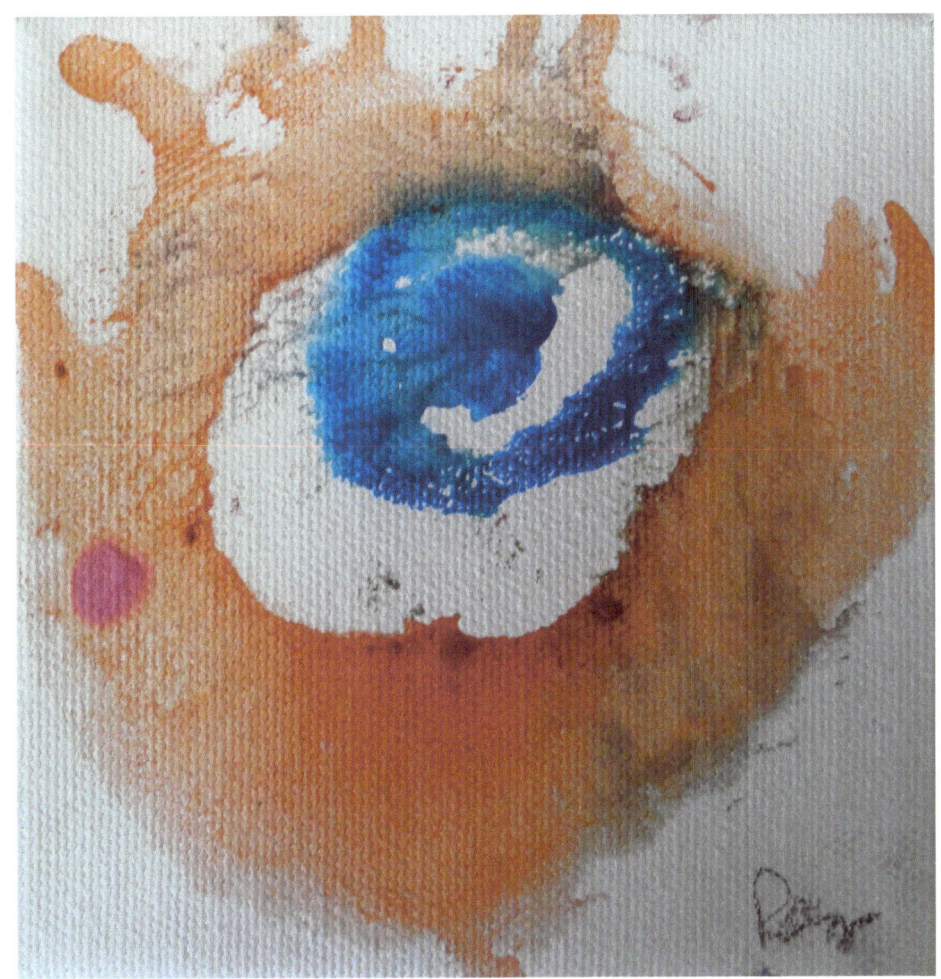

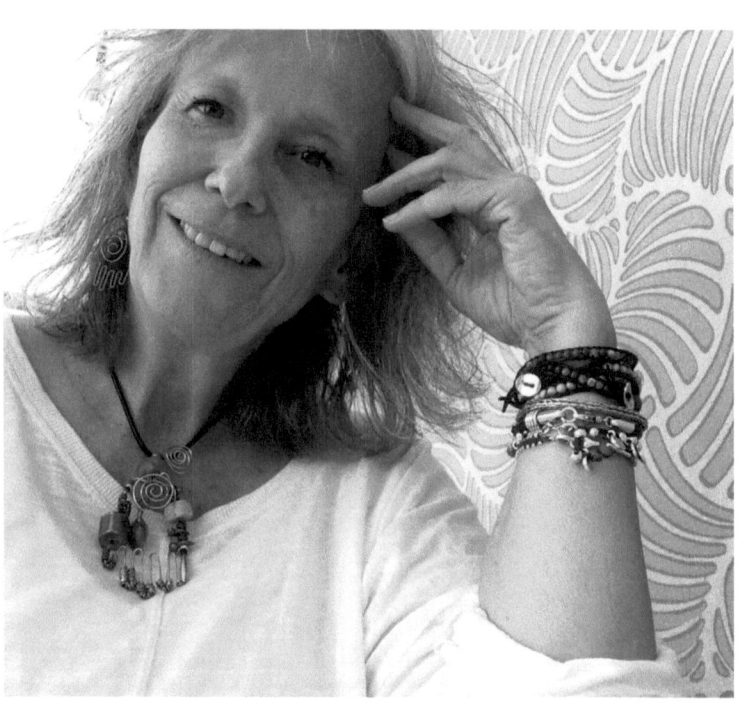

Biography

Karrie Ross, conceptual, visual Artist.

A native to Los Angeles, California, Karrie Ross was exposed to a vast range of experiences throughout her life. Her parents appreciated ART of all kinds and her childhood was rich in many ways from learning what creative balance was to how to use power tools. Karrie is a survivor. She learned to take care of herself at an early age and has been doing so for most of her life. Her art comes out of her struggles and joys of living. You might see a whimsy on the outside but on the inside there are the everyday things we all experience. Fears, insecurities along with the normal wants and needs of day-to-day living and making ends meet. Karrie's art is her way to manage the bombardment of all this… when asked "What would she do if she didn't have it?" she shook her head and responded, "I wouldn't want to try."

Karrie's art started being shown around Los Angeles in the 1980s, her purpose was to be seen, learn to talk about her art and create a collectors base. She works in both watercolor and oil as they seem "more alive" and pen & ink or pencil for her never-ending fascination with doodling.

Professional sales began in the 1990s, being represented by a High-Point Gallery that worked with the decorative industry and for the next 12 years her paintings were found hanging on the walls of hotels in Japan and New York, and commercial, residential, and retail venues such as: IDA, Macy's, FAO Schwartz, MayCo., Dillards, Sax Fifth Ave, Gladmans, Coach, JCPenney's, Khol's, FredMyers, AGI, Hirshbedner, etc. as well as displayed in high-end interior design showrooms like Baker Design at the PDC. On-air exposure: TV and cable shows CSI Miami, The Standoff, Entourage, Medium; Movies: Shadowboxer, Burn After Reading to name a few. Karrie's artwork can be found in private and corporate local, national, and international collections.

Ross' art has been featured at: the Lancaster Museum MOAH, the Brand Library, the Annual International "Ink and Clay" exhibition at the Kellogg University Art Gallery, Pomona; LA Artcore Union Center for the arts; three Museum location traveling show 2014-2015, to the grand Salone d'Ingresso of Il Palazzo della Provincia di Frosinone, Italy and at the OMA Oceanside Museum of Art and RAM Riverside Art Museum in California; the Los Angeles Municipal Arts Gallery; and interviewed by two Arts Entertainment shows, as well as exhibitions at galleries local and regional. Artslant.com, the #1 Contemporary Artist Network website, has spotlighted her work among first round Showcase winners for both painting and mixed media. She was a member of the Los Angeles Art Association, Gallery 825, for over 5yrs.

PUBLICATION: Her art and exhibitions have been written about in Cartwheel, Thrillist/LA, Hollywood Today, Topanga Messenger, Santa Monica SUN, American Chronicle, Santa Monica Mirror, the Examiner, the Los Angeles Times, the Huffington Post, to name a few.

AWARDS: Spiral Series: Energy Bloom subset have won honorable mentions in two juried art award shows and one for the Blossoms II National show. The "Portraits" series, the head of "Freedom" won an honorable mention in the 2012 Whole9 Traveling Peace Project. And "As the Cloud Weeps: Bejeweled Bird" won 3rd place in a local show in 2013. She is also an award-winning author of a non-fiction book about parenting, and childrens picture book.

KARRIE runs an award winning graphic design business (over 25 years) that specializes in the design of fiction and non-fiction books, and collateral for self publishing authors, services, products and small businesses. She consults on brand recognition, marketing, merchandising, and on how to create a web-presence. She served on the Board of Directors for the Art Directors Club of Los Angeles for 5 years in the 1980s.

In the end, Ross is about the seeing of oneself and the knowing of ones personal energy.

Her work is her on going creative exploration.

Solo Exhibitions

2014 LA Artcore Union Center for the Arts; Three Artists; Los Angeles, CA
2014 Sundance Cinema Art Gallery, West Hollywood; Spiral Series; West Hollywood, CA
2013 AlteredSpace Gallery: "Patterns"; Abbot Kinney, Three Artists. Venice Beach, CA
2006 KTGY Group, Inc. 4 month office installation, Orange County, CA
2003-2005 BGH Gallery; Bergamot Station: Santa Monica, CA

Select Museum/College/NonProfit Exhibitions

– Traveling International Show (2014-2015) "California Dreaming" An International Portrait of Southern California, Jurors: Alfio Borghese, Gallery Director of Il Palazzo della Provincia di Frosinone, Peter Frank. The exhibition will be seen at the following venues:

- Palazzo della Provincia di Frosinone, Frosinone, Italy
- Oceanside Museum of Art, OMA, Oceanside CA
- Riverside Art Museum, RAM, Riverside, CA

– Kellogg University Art Gallery: "INK & CLAY"; Jurors: Jeannie Denhol, Dave Lefner, Phyllis Green, Pamona, CA
– MOAH Museum of Art History Lancaster: "National Treasure California Poppy", Curated by Andi Campognone, Lancaster, CA
– The Brand Library – "Works on Paper #25, #30 and #42"; Juror for #42: Jack Rutberg, Glendale, CA
– Los Angeles Municipal Gallery, Barnsdale Park; Los Angeles
– Century Gallery: "Symbols/Signs", Northridge, CA

Art Fairs
– World Wide Art Fair, LA Convention Center, Art Unified, Los Angeles, CA
– LA Art Show: LA Convention Center; Fabrik; Los Angeles, CA

Select Gallery Group Exhibitions

2015 (as of April)
– The Atrium Gallery: three person show, Paso Robles, CA
– bG Gallery: Grayscale Wonderland; Bergamot Station, Santa Monica, CA
– MAS Attack 8; San Deigo, CA
– Loft at Liz's; WaterWorks I, traveling show, Los Angeles, CA
– Porch Gallery: WaterWorks II, Ojai, CA
– Homing Pigeons; Kyoto, Japan

2014
– Porch Gallery: Venice Institute of Contemporary Arts; "Water Works": Traveling show. Ojai, CA
– Studio C Gallery: Santa Fe Arts Colony: "Oneira: I Dream the Self"; Juror: Betty Brown; Los Angeles, CA
– Install: "Our Ever Changing World: Through the Eyes of Artists": One night event. Question: "What are you saving from extinction?"; Book Signing and Art Exhibit; group showing of all 36 artists in the book; Los Angeles, CA
– Topanga Canyon Gallery; Annual Show; AWARD Third Place; Juror: Jim Morphesis. Topanga, CA

2013
– Bleicher/Golightly/Gorman: "From Little Things Big Things Grow"; Santa Monica, CA
– Broadway Art Space:Group Show: "Women Make the World Go Round"; Santa Monica, CA
– The Peace Project 2013; Whole-9; one of 165 pieces that will be reproduced as 1'x1' squares for a traveling show. Culver City, CA
– Red Pipe Gallery: "City & Self"; Curated by Mat Gleason; Los Angeles, CA
– Garboushian Gallery: "MANA" Fundraiser: Curated by Lori Garboushian; Beverly Hills, CA

2012
– The Peace Project 2012; Honorable mention; Whole-9; Traveline Show, Culver City, CA
– LAX, Terminal One: "Le Petite Jardin"; Los Angeles, CA – 6mons install
– Billboard Art in two Cities: Reading, PA, and Corona, CA

2011
– Chicago Billboard Project: Ten images with the words, "Breast Awareness" . Chicago, Ill
– Pacific Art League: National Competition, Juror: JoAnne Northrup, San Jose Museum of Art, Palo Alto, CA
– Gallery 825: Annual Auction; "Oh The Two Of Us" SOLD to Mr. and Mrs. Herair Garboushian; Los Angeles, CA
– Shoshana Wayne Gallery: "Chain Letter" curated by Christian Cummings & Doug Harvey; over 1,700 artists participated—it was truly an ART Happening; Santa Monica, CA
– Gallery 825: "Not A Car"; Jurors: Silvia Sonnenschmidt and Thomas Volkmann; Los Angeles, CA

2010
– Blossoms II Award Show: AWARD: Honorable Mention awarded to Spiral Series: Energy Blooms: "We Dance"; selected from 2,300 entries; Susan Kathleen Black Foundation
– Williams-Sonoma Home; Fall Wall Decor: "Graffiti"
– TAG Gallery, "California Open" Bergamot Station; Juror: Karen Moss; Santa Monica, CA
– Santa Monica Cultural Affairs; Annenberg Beach House; Santa Monica, CA
– The Brewery Art Walk; Los Angeles, CA

1999-2009 Selected sales to the decorative industry through a gallery at High Point, Atlanta, GA

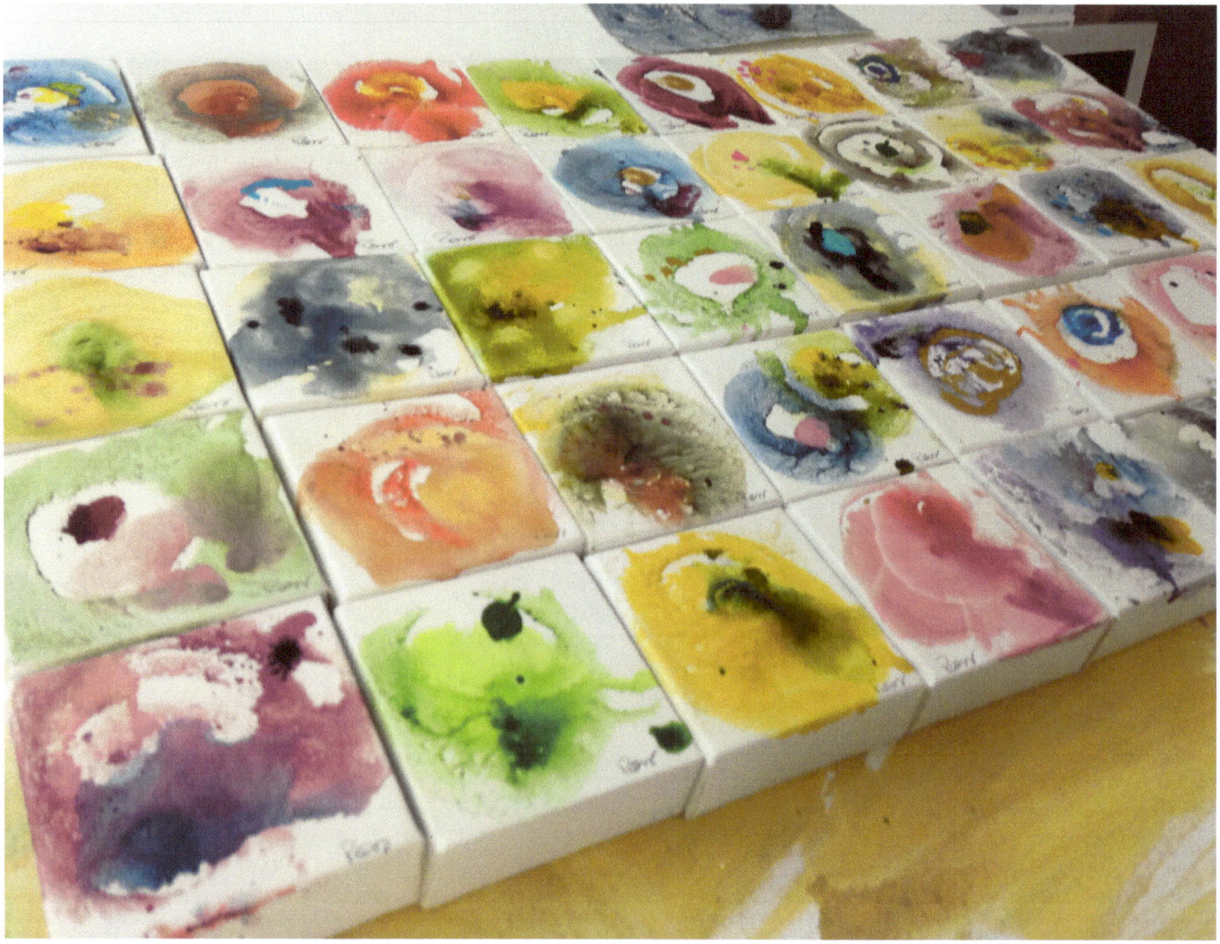

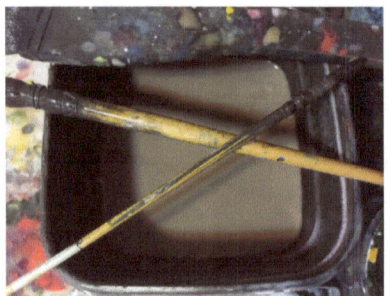

Top: 4"x4"; watercolor on canvas; sealed

Left: my brushes and water vessel

www.ingramcontent.com/pod-product-compliance
Lightning Source LLC
Chambersburg PA
CBHW050402180526

45159CB00005B/2124